Winning
By Design

Sales
Notebook

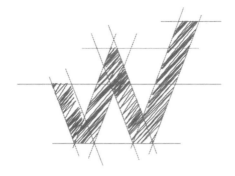

In case of loss, please return to:

....

....

....

....

Revision 5.0

ISBN-13: 978-1987730647

ISBN-10: 198773064X

Winning by Design LLC
San Francisco, California
United States of America
For more information, visit www.winningbydesign.com

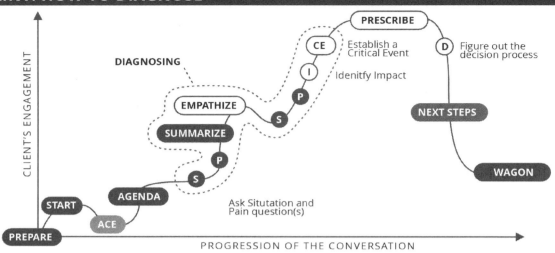

STEP	DESCRIPTION	PREP & FOLLOW-UP
OPEN	Exchange pleasantries. Ask approval to take notes/record call. Ask if they reviewed the "asset" that was included in the invite	• Review LinkedIn Profiles • Include asset in Invite
ACE	Orchestrate the call, set the end goal and engage **A** Appreciate: *Appreciate you taking the time* **C** Check time: *Are we still good for 30 minutes?* (Ask everyone) **E** Verify end goal: *Typically at the end of this call we agree to...* Ask: *Does that sound right?*	• Determine what the outcome of the meeting is
AGENDA	• Confirm the agenda • Ask attendees: *What would you like to get out of this call?* • Involve everyone: *How about you, Danny?* • Repeat: *Is there anything else?* • Ask: *What is the most important to you?* • Compartmentalize the meeting based on topics	• Send calendar invite • Include an executive brief • Multiple attendees? Ask your coach to brief you • Reconfirm at 24hrs, and again at 5 mins, before
Ask **open and closed ended questions**	• Use Closed- and Open-ended questions to *Engage* and *Pace* • Closed: *Do you have people working for you?* • Closed w/ context: *LinkedIn shows that you have 12 people in Marketing working for you...did I get that right?* • Open: *How do you communicate with each other?* • Open w/ context: *Jennifer mentioned you were using CRM "X" to communicate; have you seen the team leverage this?*	• Do your research • Prepare the first group of Situation and Pain • questions in Closed/Open format

Slow start
S > 1 Closed

Faster start **S > 2**
Closed w/ research

Speeding up
2 > 3 Open

Accelerate **2 > 4**
Open w/ research

STEP	DESCRIPTION	PREP & FOLLOW-UP
Diagnose by probing using **Situation** and **Pain** questions	Ask 2-4 **S** ituational questions, both open and closed Ask 1-2 **P** ain/problem questions	Prepare diagnostic questions and split them up into Situational and Pain questions

Identify Impact (I) (CE) Establish a Critical Event

Make a decision to go for Impact or Critical Event first?

EMPATHIZE

SUMMARIZE

Clients can kick the bucket and share a series of pain points

(P) (P) (P) Pain question(s)

Closed/Open questions allow you to get to the point faster

(S) Situational question

(S) Situational question

STEP	DESCRIPTION	PREP & FOLLOW-UP
SUMMARIZE	• Summarize So you have **S** and **S** causing you **P** • Ask *Did I get that right?*	Prepare a list of diagnostic open- and closed-ended questions
EMPATHIZE	• Empathize I hear this a lot or You are not alone • Refer to a **3rd** party *Mike, a VP like you, had the same...*	Find a case study that is relevant for your client
IMPACT	• Identify **I** mpact on the business: ↑revenue ↓cost, improve Customer Experience, User Experience *How does this impact you/your business?*	Prepare a list of possible Impacts
CRITICAL EVENT	• Establish a **C** ritical **E** vent: *When do you need this by?* • Followed by *What happens if you miss that date?*	Prepare critical events and impact that may apply
DECISION	**D** ecision – Criteria and Process: *What is the trade-off you are making... Have you brought on a solution like this before?*	Listen carefully/prepare a comparison table
NEXT STEPS	First Did we address your questions? Follow up on ACE *At the beginning of the call we said... Close May I ask, are you ready to move forward with...*	Prepare what to ask for! This should be aligned with ACE opening
WAGONS	Orchestrate outcome... • *What would you like to achieve with...* Then suggest to involve others to accomplish that.. • *Would you consider inviting...* • *Other clients similar to yourself found it beneficial to invite...*	Research the people you think should be in the next meeting
FOLLOW THROUGH	Immediately follow through with deliverables, and/or confirm in email what was discussed	Follow up immediately

Date   /   /

CUSTOMER INFO

S ITUATIONAL QUESTIONS
Use both open- and closed-ended questions

Company _____

Name/Title _____

_____

PREPARATION NOTES

P AIN QUESTIONS

3 RD-PARTY REFERENCES

Company	Customer challenge of solution
_____	_____
_____	_____
_____	_____
_____	_____

Date / /

CALL NOTES

CRITICAL EVENT

_____

_____

_____

RATIONAL IMPACT

- _____
- _____
- _____
- _____

EMOTIONAL IMPACT

- _____
- _____
- _____

FOLLOW UPS
Who/What

_____

_____

_____

_____

DECISION CRITERIA

Date   /   /

CUSTOMER INFO

Company _____

Name/Title _____

_____

PREPARATION NOTES

S ITUATIONAL QUESTIONS
Use both open- and closed-ended questions

_____

_____

_____

_____

P AIN QUESTIONS

_____

_____

_____

_____

3 RD-PARTY REFERENCES

Company	Customer challenge of solution
_____	_____
_____	_____
_____	_____

CALL NOTES

CRITICAL EVENT

_____

_____

_____

RATIONAL IMPACT

- _____
- _____
- _____
- _____

EMOTIONAL IMPACT

- _____
- _____
- _____

FOLLOW UPS
Who/What

_____

_____

_____

_____

DECISION CRITERIA

Date   /   /

CUSTOMER INFO

Company _____

Name/Title _____

_____

PREPARATION NOTES

S ITUATIONAL QUESTIONS
Use both open- and closed-ended questions

_____

_____

_____

_____

P AIN QUESTIONS

_____

_____

_____

_____

3 RD-PARTY REFERENCES

Company	Customer challenge of solution
_____	_____
_____	_____
_____	_____
_____	_____

Date / /

CALL NOTES

CRITICAL EVENT

_____

_____

_____

RATIONAL IMPACT

- _____

- _____

- _____

- _____

EMOTIONAL IMPACT

- _____

- _____

- _____

FOLLOW UPS
Who/What

_____

_____

_____

_____

DECISION CRITERIA

Date   /   /

CUSTOMER INFO

Company _____

Name/Title _____

_____

PREPARATION NOTES

S ITUATIONAL QUESTIONS
Use both open- and closed-ended questions

_____

_____

_____

_____

P AIN QUESTIONS

_____

_____

_____

_____

3 RD-PARTY REFERENCES

Company   Customer challenge of solution

_____   _____

_____   _____

_____   _____

Date   /   /

CALL NOTES

CRITICAL EVENT

_____

_____

_____

RATIONAL IMPACT

- _____

- _____

- _____

- _____

EMOTIONAL IMPACT

- _____

- _____

- _____

FOLLOW UPS
Who/What

_____

_____

_____

_____

DECISION CRITERIA

BEFORE THE CALL

Date / /

CUSTOMER INFO

Company _____

Name/Title _____

_____

PREPARATION NOTES

S ITUATIONAL QUESTIONS
Use both open- and closed-ended questions

_____

_____

_____

_____

P AIN QUESTIONS

_____

_____

_____

_____

3 RD-PARTY REFERENCES

Company	Customer challenge of solution
_____	_____
_____	_____
_____	_____

DURING THE CALL

Date   /   /

CALL NOTES

CRITICAL EVENT

_____

_____

_____

RATIONAL IMPACT

- _____

- _____

- _____

- _____

EMOTIONAL IMPACT

- _____

- _____

- _____

FOLLOW UPS

Who/What

_____

_____

_____

_____

DECISION CRITERIA

BEFORE THE CALL

Date / /

CUSTOMER INFO

Company _____

Name/Title _____

_____

PREPARATION NOTES

S ITUATIONAL QUESTIONS
Use both open- and closed-ended questions

_____

_____

_____

_____

P AIN QUESTIONS

_____

_____

_____

_____

3 RD-PARTY REFERENCES

Company	Customer challenge of solution
_____	_____
_____	_____
_____	_____
_____	_____

CALL NOTES

CRITICAL EVENT

_____

_____

_____

RATIONAL IMPACT

- _____
- _____
- _____
- _____

EMOTIONAL IMPACT

- _____
- _____
- _____

FOLLOW UPS

Who/What

_____

_____

_____

_____

DECISION CRITERIA

Date   /   /

CUSTOMER INFO

S ITUATIONAL QUESTIONS
Use both open- and closed-ended questions

Company _____

Name/Title _____

_____

PREPARATION NOTES

P AIN QUESTIONS

3 RD-PARTY REFERENCES

Company   Customer challenge of solution

_____   _____

_____   _____

_____   _____

_____   _____

Date /   /

CALL NOTES

CRITICAL EVENT

_____

_____

_____

RATIONAL IMPACT

- _____
- _____
- _____
- _____

EMOTIONAL IMPACT

- _____
- _____
- _____

FOLLOW UPS

Who/What

_____

_____

_____

_____

DECISION CRITERIA

Date / /

CUSTOMER INFO

S ITUATIONAL QUESTIONS
Use both open- and closed-ended questions

Company _____

_____

Name/Title _____

_____

_____

_____

PREPARATION NOTES

_____

P AIN QUESTIONS

_____

_____

_____

_____

3 RD-PARTY REFERENCES

Company   Customer challenge of solution

_____   _____

_____   _____

_____   _____

Date   /   /

CALL NOTES

CRITICAL EVENT

_____

_____

_____

RATIONAL IMPACT

- _____
- _____
- _____
- _____

EMOTIONAL IMPACT

- _____
- _____
- _____

FOLLOW UPS

Who/What

_____

_____

_____

_____

DECISION CRITERIA

BEFORE THE CALL

Date   /   /

CUSTOMER INFO

S ITUATIONAL QUESTIONS
Use both open- and closed-ended questions

Company _____

_____

Name/Title _____

_____

_____

_____

PREPARATION NOTES

P AIN QUESTIONS

_____

_____

_____

_____

3 RD-PARTY REFERENCES

Company	Customer challenge of solution
_____	_____
_____	_____
_____	_____

Date / /

CALL NOTES

CRITICAL EVENT

_____

_____

_____

RATIONAL IMPACT

- _____

- _____

- _____

- _____

EMOTIONAL IMPACT

- _____

- _____

- _____

FOLLOW UPS
Who/What

_____

_____

_____

_____

DECISION CRITERIA

Date / /

CUSTOMER INFO

S ITUATIONAL QUESTIONS
Use both open- and closed-ended questions

Company _____

Name/Title _____

_____

PREPARATION NOTES

P AIN QUESTIONS

3 RD-PARTY REFERENCES

Company   Customer challenge of solution

_____   _____

_____   _____

_____   _____

_____   _____

Date / /

CALL NOTES

CRITICAL EVENT

_____

_____

_____

RATIONAL IMPACT

- _____

- _____

- _____

- _____

EMOTIONAL IMPACT

- _____

- _____

- _____

FOLLOW UPS
Who/What

_____

_____

_____

_____

DECISION CRITERIA

Date   /   /

CUSTOMER INFO

Company _____

Name/Title _____

_____

PREPARATION NOTES

S ITUATIONAL QUESTIONS
Use both open- and closed-ended questions

_____

_____

_____

_____

P AIN QUESTIONS

_____

_____

_____

_____

3 RD-PARTY REFERENCES

Company	Customer challenge of solution
_____	_____
_____	_____
_____	_____
_____	_____

Date / /

CALL NOTES

FOLLOW UPS
Who/What

CRITICAL EVENT

RATIONAL IMPACT

-
-
-
-

EMOTIONAL IMPACT

-
-
-

DECISION CRITERIA

Date   /   /

CUSTOMER INFO

S ITUATIONAL QUESTIONS
Use both open- and closed-ended questions

Company _____

Name/Title _____

_____

PREPARATION NOTES

P AIN QUESTIONS

3 RD-PARTY REFERENCES

Company   Customer challenge of solution

Date / /

CALL NOTES

CRITICAL EVENT

_____

_____

_____

RATIONAL IMPACT

- _____
- _____
- _____
- _____

EMOTIONAL IMPACT

- _____
- _____
- _____

FOLLOW UPS

Who/What

_____

_____

_____

_____

DECISION CRITERIA

Date   /   /

CUSTOMER INFO

S ITUATIONAL QUESTIONS
Use both open- and closed-ended questions

Company _____

_____

Name/Title _____

_____

_____

_____

PREPARATION NOTES

_____

P AIN QUESTIONS

_____

_____

_____

_____

3 RD-PARTY REFERENCES

Company   Customer challenge of solution

_____   _____

_____   _____

_____   _____

_____   _____

Date / /

CALL NOTES

CRITICAL EVENT

_____

_____

_____

RATIONAL IMPACT

- _____

- _____

- _____

- _____

EMOTIONAL IMPACT

- _____

- _____

- _____

FOLLOW UPS
Who/What

_____

_____

_____

_____

DECISION CRITERIA

31

Date   /   /

CUSTOMER INFO

S ITUATIONAL QUESTIONS
Use both open- and closed-ended questions

Company _____

_____

Name/Title _____

_____

_____

_____

PREPARATION NOTES

_____

P AIN QUESTIONS

_____

_____

_____

_____

3 RD-PARTY REFERENCES

Company   Customer challenge of solution

_____   _____

_____   _____

_____   _____

_____   _____

CALL NOTES

CRITICAL EVENT

_____

_____

_____

RATIONAL IMPACT

- _____

- _____

- _____

- _____

EMOTIONAL IMPACT

- _____

- _____

- _____

FOLLOW UPS
Who/What

_____

_____

_____

_____

DECISION CRITERIA

Date   /   /

CUSTOMER INFO

S ITUATIONAL QUESTIONS
Use both open- and closed-ended questions

Company _____

Name/Title _____

_____

PREPARATION NOTES

P AIN QUESTIONS

3 RD-PARTY REFERENCES

Company   Customer challenge of solution

_____   _____

_____   _____

_____   _____

Date / /

CALL NOTES

CRITICAL EVENT

_____

_____

_____

RATIONAL IMPACT

- _____
- _____
- _____
- _____

EMOTIONAL IMPACT

- _____
- _____
- _____

FOLLOW UPS

Who/What

_____

_____

_____

_____

DECISION CRITERIA

Date   /   /

CUSTOMER INFO

S ITUATIONAL QUESTIONS
Use both open- and closed-ended questions

Company _____

Name/Title _____

_____

PREPARATION NOTES

P AIN QUESTIONS

3 RD-PARTY REFERENCES

Company   Customer challenge of solution

Date   /   /

CALL NOTES

CRITICAL EVENT

_____

_____

_____

RATIONAL IMPACT

- _____
- _____
- _____
- _____

EMOTIONAL IMPACT

- _____
- _____
- _____

FOLLOW UPS

Who/What

_____

_____

_____

_____

DECISION CRITERIA

BEFORE THE CALL

Date   /   /

CUSTOMER INFO

S ITUATIONAL QUESTIONS
Use both open- and closed-ended questions

Company _____

Name/Title _____

_____

PREPARATION NOTES

P AIN QUESTIONS

3 RD-PARTY REFERENCES

Company   Customer challenge of solution

_____   _____

_____   _____

_____   _____

_____   _____

Date / /

CALL NOTES

CRITICAL EVENT

_____

_____

_____

RATIONAL IMPACT

- _____
- _____
- _____
- _____

EMOTIONAL IMPACT

- _____
- _____
- _____

FOLLOW UPS

Who/What

_____

_____

_____

_____

DECISION CRITERIA

Date   /   /

CUSTOMER INFO

S ITUATIONAL QUESTIONS
Use both open- and closed-ended questions

Company _____

Name/Title _____

_____

PREPARATION NOTES

P AIN QUESTIONS

3 RD-PARTY REFERENCES

Company   Customer challenge of solution

Date   /   /

CALL NOTES

CRITICAL EVENT

_____

_____

_____

RATIONAL IMPACT

- _____
- _____
- _____
- _____

EMOTIONAL IMPACT

- _____
- _____
- _____

FOLLOW UPS

Who/What

_____

_____

_____

_____

DECISION CRITERIA

Date   /   /

CUSTOMER INFO

S ITUATIONAL QUESTIONS
Use both open- and closed-ended questions

Company _____   _____

Name/Title _____   _____

_____   _____

PREPARATION NOTES   _____

P AIN QUESTIONS

_____

_____

_____

_____

3 RD-PARTY REFERENCES

Company   Customer challenge of solution

_____   _____

_____   _____

_____   _____

DURING THE CALL

Date / /

CALL NOTES

CRITICAL EVENT

_____
_____
_____

RATIONAL IMPACT

- _____
- _____
- _____
- _____

EMOTIONAL IMPACT

- _____
- _____
- _____

FOLLOW UPS
Who/What

DECISION CRITERIA

43

CUSTOMER INFO

S ITUATIONAL QUESTIONS
Use both open- and closed-ended questions

Company _____

_____

Name/Title _____

_____

_____

_____

PREPARATION NOTES

_____

P AIN QUESTIONS

_____

_____

_____

_____

3 RD-PARTY REFERENCES

Company   Customer challenge of solution

_____   _____

_____   _____

_____   _____

_____   _____

Date   /   /

CALL NOTES

CRITICAL EVENT

_____

_____

_____

RATIONAL IMPACT

- _____

- _____

- _____

- _____

EMOTIONAL IMPACT

- _____

- _____

- _____

FOLLOW UPS
Who/What

_____

_____

_____

_____

DECISION CRITERIA

Date   /   /

CUSTOMER INFO

S ITUATIONAL QUESTIONS
Use both open- and closed-ended questions

Company _____

_____

Name/Title _____

_____

_____

_____

PREPARATION NOTES

_____

P AIN QUESTIONS

_____

_____

_____

_____

3 RD-PARTY REFERENCES

Company   Customer challenge of solution

_____   _____

_____   _____

_____   _____

_____   _____

CALL NOTES

CRITICAL EVENT

_____
_____
_____

RATIONAL IMPACT

- _____
- _____
- _____
- _____

EMOTIONAL IMPACT

- _____
- _____
- _____

FOLLOW UPS
Who/What

_____

_____

_____

_____

DECISION CRITERIA

CUSTOMER INFO

S ITUATIONAL QUESTIONS
Use both open- and closed-ended questions

Company _____

Name/Title _____

_____

PREPARATION NOTES

P AIN QUESTIONS

3 RD-PARTY REFERENCES

Company   Customer challenge of solution

_____   _____

_____   _____

_____   _____

_____   _____

DURING THE CALL

Date / /

CALL NOTES

CRITICAL EVENT

RATIONAL IMPACT

-
-
-
-

EMOTIONAL IMPACT

-
-
-

FOLLOW UPS
Who/What

DECISION CRITERIA

Date   /   /

CUSTOMER INFO

S ITUATIONAL QUESTIONS
Use both open- and closed-ended questions

Company _____

Name/Title _____

_____

PREPARATION NOTES

P AIN QUESTIONS

3 RD-PARTY REFERENCES

Company   Customer challenge of solution

CALL NOTES

CRITICAL EVENT

_____
_____
_____

RATIONAL IMPACT

- _____
- _____
- _____
- _____

EMOTIONAL IMPACT

- _____
- _____
- _____

FOLLOW UPS
Who/What

_____
_____
_____
_____

DECISION CRITERIA

BEFORE THE CALL

CUSTOMER INFO

S ITUATIONAL QUESTIONS
Use both open- and closed-ended questions

Company _____

_____

Name/Title _____

_____

_____

_____

PREPARATION NOTES

P AIN QUESTIONS

_____

_____

_____

_____

3 RD-PARTY REFERENCES

Company   Customer challenge of solution

_____   _____

_____   _____

_____   _____

_____   _____

Date / /

CALL NOTES

CRITICAL EVENT

_____
_____
_____

RATIONAL IMPACT

- _____
- _____
- _____
- _____

EMOTIONAL IMPACT

- _____
- _____
- _____

FOLLOW UPS

Who/What

_____
_____
_____
_____

DECISION CRITERIA

BEFORE THE CALL

Date / /

CUSTOMER INFO

Company _____

Name/Title _____

_____

PREPARATION NOTES

S ITUATIONAL QUESTIONS
Use both open- and closed-ended questions

_____

_____

_____

_____

P AIN QUESTIONS

_____

_____

_____

_____

3 RD-PARTY REFERENCES

Company	Customer challenge of solution
_____	_____
_____	_____
_____	_____

CALL NOTES

CRITICAL EVENT

_____

_____

_____

RATIONAL IMPACT

- _____

- _____

- _____

- _____

EMOTIONAL IMPACT

- _____

- _____

- _____

FOLLOW UPS

Who/What

_____

_____

_____

_____

_____

DECISION CRITERIA

Date / /

CUSTOMER INFO

S ITUATIONAL QUESTIONS
Use both open- and closed-ended questions

Company _____

Name/Title _____

_____

PREPARATION NOTES

P AIN QUESTIONS

3 RD-PARTY REFERENCES

Company   Customer challenge of solution

_____   _____

_____   _____

_____   _____

Date / /

CALL NOTES

CRITICAL EVENT

_____

_____

_____

RATIONAL IMPACT

- _____
- _____
- _____
- _____

EMOTIONAL IMPACT

- _____
- _____
- _____

FOLLOW UPS

Who/What

_____

_____

_____

_____

DECISION CRITERIA

BEFORE THE CALL

Date / /

CUSTOMER INFO

Company _____

Name/Title _____

_____

PREPARATION NOTES

[S] ITUATIONAL QUESTIONS
Use both open- and closed-ended questions

_____

_____

_____

_____

[P] AIN QUESTIONS

_____

_____

_____

_____

[3] RD-PARTY REFERENCES

Company	Customer challenge of solution
_____	_____
_____	_____
_____	_____

Date /   /

CALL NOTES

CRITICAL EVENT

_____

_____

_____

RATIONAL IMPACT

- _____

- _____

- _____

- _____

EMOTIONAL IMPACT

- _____

- _____

- _____

FOLLOW UPS

Who/What

DECISION CRITERIA

_____

_____

_____

_____

Date /   /

CUSTOMER INFO

Company _____

Name/Title _____

_____

PREPARATION NOTES

S ITUATIONAL QUESTIONS
Use both open- and closed-ended questions

_____

_____

_____

_____

P AIN QUESTIONS

_____

_____

_____

_____

3 RD-PARTY REFERENCES

Company   Customer challenge of solution

_____   _____

_____   _____

_____   _____

_____   _____

Date / /

CALL NOTES

CRITICAL EVENT

_____
_____
_____

RATIONAL IMPACT

- _____
- _____
- _____
- _____

EMOTIONAL IMPACT

- _____
- _____
- _____

FOLLOW UPS

Who/What

_____

_____

_____

_____

DECISION CRITERIA

Date   /   /

CUSTOMER INFO

S ITUATIONAL QUESTIONS
Use both open- and closed-ended questions

Company _____

Name/Title _____

_____

PREPARATION NOTES

P AIN QUESTIONS

3 RD-PARTY REFERENCES

Company	Customer challenge of solution

Date   /   /

CALL NOTES

CRITICAL EVENT

_____

_____

_____

RATIONAL IMPACT

- _____

- _____

- _____

- _____

EMOTIONAL IMPACT

- _____

- _____

- _____

FOLLOW UPS

Who/What

DECISION CRITERIA

Date / /

CUSTOMER INFO

S ITUATIONAL QUESTIONS
Use both open- and closed-ended questions

Company _____

_____

Name/Title _____

_____

_____

_____

PREPARATION NOTES

P AIN QUESTIONS

_____

_____

_____

_____

3 RD-PARTY REFERENCES

Company   Customer challenge of solution

_____   _____

_____   _____

_____   _____

Date / /

CALL NOTES

CRITICAL EVENT

_____

_____

_____

RATIONAL IMPACT

- _____
- _____
- _____
- _____

EMOTIONAL IMPACT

- _____
- _____
- _____

FOLLOW UPS
Who/What

_____

_____

_____

_____

DECISION CRITERIA

Date / /

CUSTOMER INFO

S ITUATIONAL QUESTIONS
Use both open- and closed-ended questions

Company _____

Name/Title _____

_____

PREPARATION NOTES

P AIN QUESTIONS

3 RD-PARTY REFERENCES

Company   Customer challenge of solution

_____   _____

_____   _____

_____   _____

CALL NOTES

CRITICAL EVENT

_____

_____

_____

RATIONAL IMPACT

- _____

- _____

- _____

- _____

EMOTIONAL IMPACT

- _____

- _____

- _____

FOLLOW UPS

Who/What

_____

_____

_____

_____

DECISION CRITERIA

Date / /

CUSTOMER INFO

S ITUATIONAL QUESTIONS
Use both open- and closed-ended questions

Company _____

Name/Title _____

_____

PREPARATION NOTES

P AIN QUESTIONS

3 RD-PARTY REFERENCES

Company   Customer challenge of solution

_____   _____

_____   _____

_____   _____

Date / /

CALL NOTES

CRITICAL EVENT

_____

_____

_____

RATIONAL IMPACT

- _____
- _____
- _____
- _____

EMOTIONAL IMPACT

- _____
- _____
- _____

FOLLOW UPS
Who/What

_____

_____

_____

_____

DECISION CRITERIA

Date / /

CUSTOMER INFO

S ITUATIONAL QUESTIONS
Use both open- and closed-ended questions

Company _____

Name/Title _____

PREPARATION NOTES

P AIN QUESTIONS

3 RD-PARTY REFERENCES

Company   Customer challenge of solution

_____   _____

_____   _____

_____   _____

_____   _____

Date / /

CALL NOTES

CRITICAL EVENT

_____

_____

_____

RATIONAL IMPACT

- _____
- _____
- _____
- _____

EMOTIONAL IMPACT

- _____
- _____
- _____

FOLLOW UPS

Who/What

_____

_____

_____

_____

DECISION CRITERIA

Date   /   /

CUSTOMER INFO

S ITUATIONAL QUESTIONS
Use both open- and closed-ended questions

Company _____

Name/Title _____

_____

PREPARATION NOTES

P AIN QUESTIONS

3 RD-PARTY REFERENCES

Company   Customer challenge of solution

_____   _____

_____   _____

_____   _____

Date /   /

CALL NOTES

CRITICAL EVENT

_____

_____

_____

RATIONAL IMPACT

- _____
- _____
- _____
- _____

EMOTIONAL IMPACT

- _____
- _____
- _____

FOLLOW UPS
Who/What

_____

_____

_____

_____

DECISION CRITERIA

CUSTOMER INFO

S ITUATIONAL QUESTIONS
Use both open- and closed-ended questions

Company _____

Name/Title _____

_____

PREPARATION NOTES

P AIN QUESTIONS

3 RD-PARTY REFERENCES

Company   Customer challenge of solution

_____   _____

_____   _____

_____   _____

Date / /

CALL NOTES

CRITICAL EVENT

_____

_____

_____

RATIONAL IMPACT

- _____
- _____
- _____
- _____

EMOTIONAL IMPACT

- _____
- _____
- _____

FOLLOW UPS

Who/What

_____

_____

_____

_____

DECISION CRITERIA

Date ___ / ___ / ___

CUSTOMER INFO

S ITUATIONAL QUESTIONS
Use both open- and closed-ended questions

Company _____

Name/Title _____

_____

PREPARATION NOTES

P AIN QUESTIONS

3 RD-PARTY REFERENCES

Company   Customer challenge of solution

_____   _____

_____   _____

_____   _____

_____   _____

Date / /

CALL NOTES

CRITICAL EVENT

_____

_____

_____

RATIONAL IMPACT

- _____

- _____

- _____

- _____

EMOTIONAL IMPACT

- _____

- _____

- _____

FOLLOW UPS

Who/What

_____

_____

_____

_____

DECISION CRITERIA

BEFORE THE CALL

Date / /

CUSTOMER INFO

Company _____

Name/Title _____

_____

PREPARATION NOTES

S ITUATIONAL QUESTIONS
Use both open- and closed-ended questions

_____

_____

_____

_____

P AIN QUESTIONS

_____

_____

_____

_____

3 RD-PARTY REFERENCES

Company   Customer challenge of solution

_____   _____

_____   _____

_____   _____

Date / /

CALL NOTES

CRITICAL EVENT

_____

_____

_____

RATIONAL IMPACT

- _____

- _____

- _____

- _____

EMOTIONAL IMPACT

- _____

- _____

- _____

FOLLOW UPS

Who/What

_____

_____

_____

_____

DECISION CRITERIA

Date   /   /

CUSTOMER INFO

Company _____

Name/Title _____

_____

PREPARATION NOTES

S ITUATIONAL QUESTIONS
Use both open- and closed-ended questions

_____

_____

_____

_____

P AIN QUESTIONS

_____

_____

_____

_____

3 RD-PARTY REFERENCES

Company	Customer challenge of solution
_____	_____
_____	_____
_____	_____

CALL NOTES

CRITICAL EVENT

_____
_____
_____

RATIONAL IMPACT

- _____
- _____
- _____
- _____

EMOTIONAL IMPACT

- _____
- _____
- _____

FOLLOW UPS

Who/What

_____

_____

_____

_____

DECISION CRITERIA

Date   /   /

CUSTOMER INFO

Company _____

Name/Title _____

_____

PREPARATION NOTES

Use both open- and closed-ended questions

_____

_____

_____

_____

_____

P AIN QUESTIONS

_____

_____

_____

_____

3 RD-PARTY REFERENCES

Company	Customer challenge of solution
_____	_____
_____	_____
_____	_____

Date /   /

CALL NOTES

CRITICAL EVENT

_____

_____

_____

RATIONAL IMPACT

- _____

- _____

- _____

- _____

EMOTIONAL IMPACT

- _____

- _____

- _____

FOLLOW UPS

Who/What

DECISION CRITERIA

Date   /   /

CUSTOMER INFO

S ITUATIONAL QUESTIONS
Use both open- and closed-ended questions

Company _____

Name/Title _____

_____

PREPARATION NOTES

P AIN QUESTIONS

3 RD-PARTY REFERENCES

Company   Customer challenge of solution

Date / /

CALL NOTES

CRITICAL EVENT

_____

_____

_____

RATIONAL IMPACT

- _____
- _____
- _____
- _____

EMOTIONAL IMPACT

- _____
- _____
- _____

FOLLOW UPS

Who/What

_____

_____

_____

_____

DECISION CRITERIA

Date / /

CUSTOMER INFO

S ITUATIONAL QUESTIONS
Use both open- and closed-ended questions

Company _____

Name/Title _____

_____

PREPARATION NOTES

P AIN QUESTIONS

3 RD-PARTY REFERENCES

Company   Customer challenge of solution

_____   _____

_____   _____

_____   _____

Date / /

CALL NOTES

CRITICAL EVENT

_____

_____

_____

RATIONAL IMPACT

- _____
- _____
- _____
- _____

EMOTIONAL IMPACT

- _____
- _____
- _____

FOLLOW UPS

Who/What

DECISION CRITERIA

Date   /   /

CUSTOMER INFO

S ITUATIONAL QUESTIONS
Use both open- and closed-ended questions

Company _____

Name/Title _____

_____

PREPARATION NOTES

P AIN QUESTIONS

3 RD-PARTY REFERENCES

Company   Customer challenge of solution

_____   _____

_____   _____

_____   _____

DURING THE CALL

Date / /

CALL NOTES

FOLLOW UPS
Who/What

CRITICAL EVENT

RATIONAL IMPACT

-
-
-
-

EMOTIONAL IMPACT

-
-
-

DECISION CRITERIA

BEFORE THE CALL

CUSTOMER INFO

Company _____

Name/Title _____

_____

PREPARATION NOTES

S ITUATIONAL QUESTIONS
Use both open- and closed-ended questions

_____

_____

_____

_____

P AIN QUESTIONS

_____

_____

_____

_____

3 RD-PARTY REFERENCES

Company	Customer challenge of solution
_____	_____
_____	_____
_____	_____

Date / /

CALL NOTES

CRITICAL EVENT

_____
_____
_____

RATIONAL IMPACT

- _____
- _____
- _____
- _____

EMOTIONAL IMPACT

- _____
- _____
- _____

FOLLOW UPS
Who/What

_____

_____

_____

_____

DECISION CRITERIA

BEFORE THE CALL

CUSTOMER INFO

S ITUATIONAL QUESTIONS
Use both open- and closed-ended questions

Company _____

Name/Title _____

_____

PREPARATION NOTES

P AIN QUESTIONS

3 RD-PARTY REFERENCES

Company	Customer challenge of solution
_____	_____
_____	_____
_____	_____

Date / /

CALL NOTES

CRITICAL EVENT

_____

_____

_____

RATIONAL IMPACT

- _____

- _____

- _____

- _____

EMOTIONAL IMPACT

- _____

- _____

- _____

FOLLOW UPS
Who/What

DECISION CRITERIA

_____

_____

_____

_____

Date ___ / ___ / ___

CUSTOMER INFO

S ITUATIONAL QUESTIONS
Use both open- and closed-ended questions

Company _____

Name/Title _____

_____

PREPARATION NOTES

P AIN QUESTIONS

3 RD-PARTY REFERENCES

Company   Customer challenge of solution

CALL NOTES

CRITICAL EVENT

_____
_____
_____

RATIONAL IMPACT

- _____
- _____
- _____
- _____

EMOTIONAL IMPACT

- _____
- _____
- _____

FOLLOW UPS
Who/What

_____
_____
_____
_____

DECISION CRITERIA

Date   /   /

CUSTOMER INFO

Company _____

Name/Title _____

_____

PREPARATION NOTES

[ ]

S ITUATIONAL QUESTIONS
Use both open- and closed-ended questions

_____

_____

_____

_____

_____

P AIN QUESTIONS

_____

_____

_____

_____

3 RD-PARTY REFERENCES

Company	Customer challenge of solution
_____	_____
_____	_____
_____	_____

Date / /

CALL NOTES

CRITICAL EVENT

_____

_____

_____

RATIONAL IMPACT

- _____

- _____

- _____

- _____

EMOTIONAL IMPACT

- _____

- _____

- _____

FOLLOW UPS

Who/What

_____

_____

_____

_____

DECISION CRITERIA

Date   /   /

CUSTOMER INFO

S ITUATIONAL QUESTIONS
Use both open- and closed-ended questions

Company _____

Name/Title _____

_____

PREPARATION NOTES

P AIN QUESTIONS

3 RD-PARTY REFERENCES

Company   Customer challenge of solution

_____   _____

_____   _____

_____   _____

CALL NOTES

CRITICAL EVENT

_____

_____

_____

RATIONAL IMPACT

- _____
- _____
- _____
- _____

EMOTIONAL IMPACT

- _____
- _____
- _____

FOLLOW UPS
Who/What

_____

_____

_____

_____

DECISION CRITERIA

Made in the USA
Monee, IL
08 March 2022